Activities, ~~~~~ & More

The Wonderful Colorful
WONDER WHEEL
of COLOR

Lynn Koolish,

Kerry Graham &

Mary Wruck

FunStitch
STUDIO

stitch your art out.

Publisher
Amy Marson
(She's in charge of everything and everyone.)

Creative Director
Gailen Runge
(She's in charge of the people who make the books.)

Art Director Kristy Zacharias
(She's in charge of all the art in all the books.)

Business Development Manager Mary Wruck
(This book was her idea.)

Editor Lynn Koolish
(She made sure the words were correct.)

Book Designer Kerry Graham
(She made the book look the way it looks.)

Production Coordinator Zinnia Heinzmann
(She made sure the book went to the printer.)

Production Editor Katie Van Amburg
(She made sure all the words and images worked together.)

Illustrator Kerry Graham
(She made all the drawings that you see in this book.)

Editorial Photographer Nissa Brehmer*
(She took all the wonderful styled pictures that you see in this book.)

Instructional Photographer Diane Pedersen*
(She took all the wonderful instructional pictures that you see in this book.)

Photo Assistant Mary Peyton Peppo
(She helps Nissa and Diane with all the photography.)

* unless otherwise noted in the fine print

This book is brought to you by FunStitch Studio, an imprint of C&T Publishing, Inc., P.O. Box 1456, Lafayette, CA 94549.

Library of Congress Cataloging-in-Publication Data

Koolish, Lynn.

The wonderful colorful wonder wheel of color : activities, stickers, poster & more / Lynn Koolish, Kerry Graham, and Mary Wruck.

pages cm

Audience: 8 and up.

ISBN 978-1-60705-892-2 (soft cover)

1. Colors--Juvenile literature. 2. Colors--Experiments--Juvenile literature. I. Graham, Kerry, 1971- II. Wruck, Mary, 1966- III. Title.

QC495.5.K66 2014

535.6--dc23

2013043255

Printed in China

10 9 8 7 6 5 4 3 2 1

HERE'S WHAT THE FINE PRINT MEANS:

Copyright means that when someone writes something, draws or paints a picture, or even takes a photo, that person owns the "rights" to what he or she created. No one else can use those exact words or images without getting permission. That means it's not okay to copy anything that you see on the Internet or that has been published, unless you ask the creator if it's okay. For this book, we're saying it's okay to copy certain pages that are labeled "Trace or copy this page to use again and again."

CONTENTS

BONUS

- Certificate of COLOR-ology
- Extra worksheet pages
- Color stickers
- Color wheel poster

What's in this book?

This book is full of information and activities that will make you a color expert so you'll be confident when picking colors for sewing, art, and crafting projects; when decorating your room; and even when you get dressed in the morning.

READ ALL THE INSTRUCTIONS!
Read all the instructions before you begin an activity. That way you'll know what to do and how the supplies will be used.

THINGS TO KNOW >>>>>>

HAVE FUN! Don't be afraid to try any of the things in this book even if you aren't sure what to do—just try them and see what you get. Start at the beginning of the book and earn stickers for each activity, game, and puzzle. By the end of the book, you'll have earned your very own Certificate of COLOR-ology!

There may be a few things that you will need help with from a parent or other adult. Just look for the **ASK FOR HELP** symbol.

It's so much fun to play with color! We know you'll want to do the activities more than once, so there are extra worksheets at the back of the book that you can tear out and use. You can also **TRACE OR COPY** the worksheet pages as many times as you like. Access to a copy machine is recommended so you can make copies of the activity pages.

BE NEAT! You'll be using paints, markers, colored water, and other things that can be messy. Work in an area where it's okay for you to use these things. When you're using paint and other liquids, put newspaper or plastic on your worktable.

REMEMBER—only copy the pages with this label:

OK

Trace or copy this page to use again and again.

4

FRONT

BACK

COLOR WHEEL POSTER AND STICKERS

At the back of the book is a color wheel poster that you can take out of the book. The front is all colored in, but you get to color the back! Try coloring your ocean friends to match the color wheel on the front of your poster.

Hang your poster wherever you do your crafting or in your bedroom (use it when you pick out what to wear), or maybe take it to school to share with your teachers and friends. You can make a copy of your ocean picture to hang up, too.

Use the stickers at the back of the book to track your progress on your Certificate of COLOR-ology. You can use the bonus stickers any way you like.

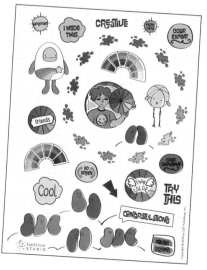

It's more fun when you learn new things with a friend. Team up with a buddy! You can work through your books together, and each of you will earn your Certificate of COLOR-ology.

5

THINGS YOU'LL NEED:

- Colored pencils
- Markers
- Crayons
- Watercolor paints
- Finger paints
- Poster paints
- Acrylic paints
- Fabric paints
- Food coloring
- Permanent markers, such as Sharpies
- Rubbing alcohol

NOTE: You don't need **all** of the listed supplies for each project! Some will work better than others for some of the activities in this book. We'll let you know what we suggest. If your activity isn't turning out as you hoped, you just might need to try something else on the list.

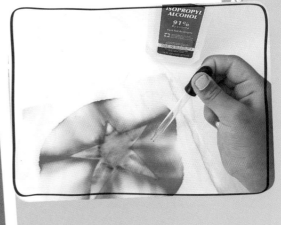

THINGS YOU MAY NEED:

- Paper
- Paintbrushes
- Tissue paper
- Chenille stems (pipe cleaners)
- Old magazines to cut up
- Paper or plastic plates
- Paper towels
- Jars for water
- Apron or old clothes to wear
- Fabric or felt
- Embroidery floss
- Basic sewing supplies, including sewing needles, pins, scissors, and an iron

Take a look around the house and see what you have on hand. For some of the activities, you may need to take a trip to a craft or art supply store, or maybe even a fabric or hardware store.

What is color?

Color is all around; everything you see is in color. Think about all the colors you see every day. What does color tell you?

Colors help set a mood or tell a story because different colors say different things. For example, bright colors are usually exciting, dark colors are stormy or dramatic, and pale colors are gentle.

Think about the time of day or season of the year. What about the colors of the foods you eat? The colors of the clothes you wear?

Look around. What do you see? How does it make you feel? Write a color story.

Why do we see color?

The "white" light that we see from the sun is actually made up of the colors red, orange, yellow, green, blue, and violet. When you see a rainbow or when light shines through a **prism**, you can see the colors.

"White" light

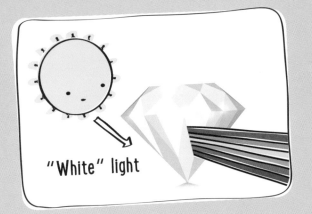
"White" light

How does the eye see color?

Now, let's look at what happens when you see something, say, a blue book. The "white" light from the sun shines on the surface of the book. All the colors in the light **except** blue are absorbed. The blue is reflected back at you, so you see blue.

ACTIVITY
How the eye sees color

TRY THIS

EARN YOUR STICKER

Draw and color your own picture of light from the sun hitting a yellow lemon or a blue bird.

YOU'LL NEED:
- Paper
- Markers, colored pencils, or crayons

DID YOU KNOW . . . ?
>>>>>> Not everyone sees colors the same.

You may see a color as red-violet and your friend may see it as blue-violet. Some people can't see the difference between red and green. To them, the colors look the same.

It's not that you have a different name for a color—for example, purple and violet are the same color with two different names. It's that you see the colors differently.

> Look at these pictures.

> What do you see in the circle and speech bubble?

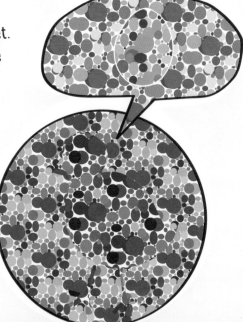

MEET ROY G. BV

R O Y G B V
Red Orange Yellow Green Blue Violet

ROY G. BV is a **mnemonic** (pronounced nih-mah-nik): an easy way to remember something.

In this case it's the order of the colors in the rainbow or on a color wheel.

TRY THIS

EARN YOUR STICKER

ACTIVITY
Color your own Roy G. BV

Use the colors of the rainbow to color in your own Roy G. BV.

YOU'LL NEED:
- Paper
- Markers, colored pencils, or crayons

OK

Trace or copy this page to use again and again.

The color wheel

What is a color wheel?

A <u>color wheel</u> is a drawing with the colors placed in a circle or a ring. It is used by students, teachers, artists, people who sew or make crafts, architects, gardeners, web designers, house painters, and anyone else who uses color—people like you!

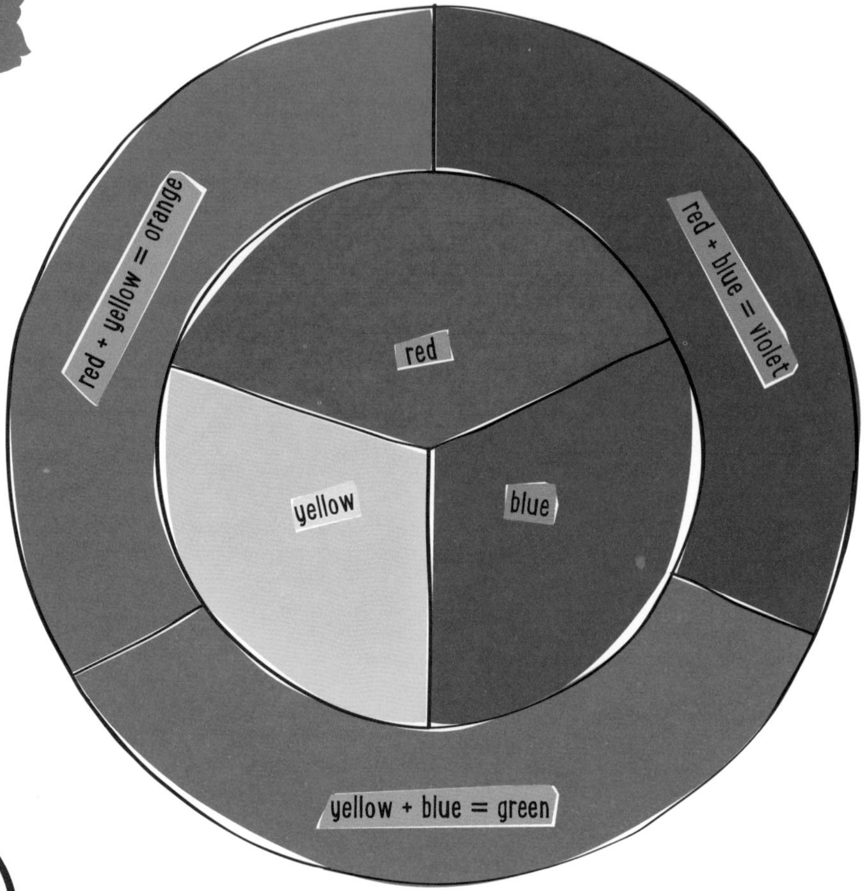

red + yellow = orange

red + blue = violet

red

yellow

blue

yellow + blue = green

Emma made this tote using a crayon transfer technique, shown on page 37.

As you read this book and do the activities, you'll find out more about how to use a color wheel and why it's so great. We bet that you, like Emma, will start using the color wheel for all sorts of things: a tote like this, or fun shoes and shirts using Sharpie art (which you'll learn about on page 16).

>>>>>> THE HISTORY OF THE COLOR WHEEL

It is said that the first color wheel was made by Sir Isaac Newton, who lived in England from 1642 to 1727. (He was a very famous scientist who brought us many scientific principles, including gravity.) After seeing how the colors separated when light passed through a prism, he arranged the colors on a disk. When the disk was spun fast enough, the colors blurred together so they looked white. This disk was the first known color wheel.

MORE FUN COLOR WHEELS

mosaic stepping stone

colored pencils

embroidery hoop

Primary colors

Three of the colors on the color wheel are very special because they are used to make or mix other colors. The colors are <u>red</u>, <u>yellow</u>, and <u>blue</u>, and they are called the <u>primary colors</u>, or <u>primaries</u>.

Secondary colors

The other three colors on this color wheel are made or mixed from the primary colors. The colors are <u>green</u>, <u>orange</u>, and <u>violet</u>, and they are called the <u>secondary colors</u>, or <u>secondaries</u>.

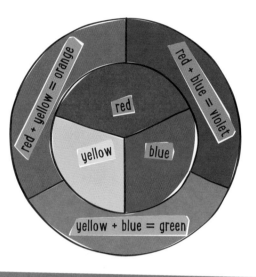

ACTIVITY
Make a torn-paper color wheel

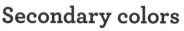

Tear old magazine pictures in primary and secondary colors and glue them on the color wheel from the next page or the worksheet page called Primary and Secondary Colors.

YOU'LL NEED:
- Paper
- Old magazines
- Scissors
- Glue

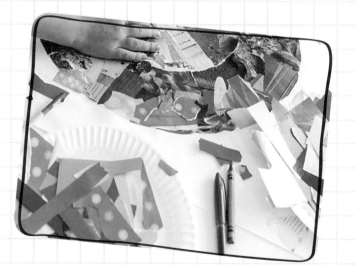

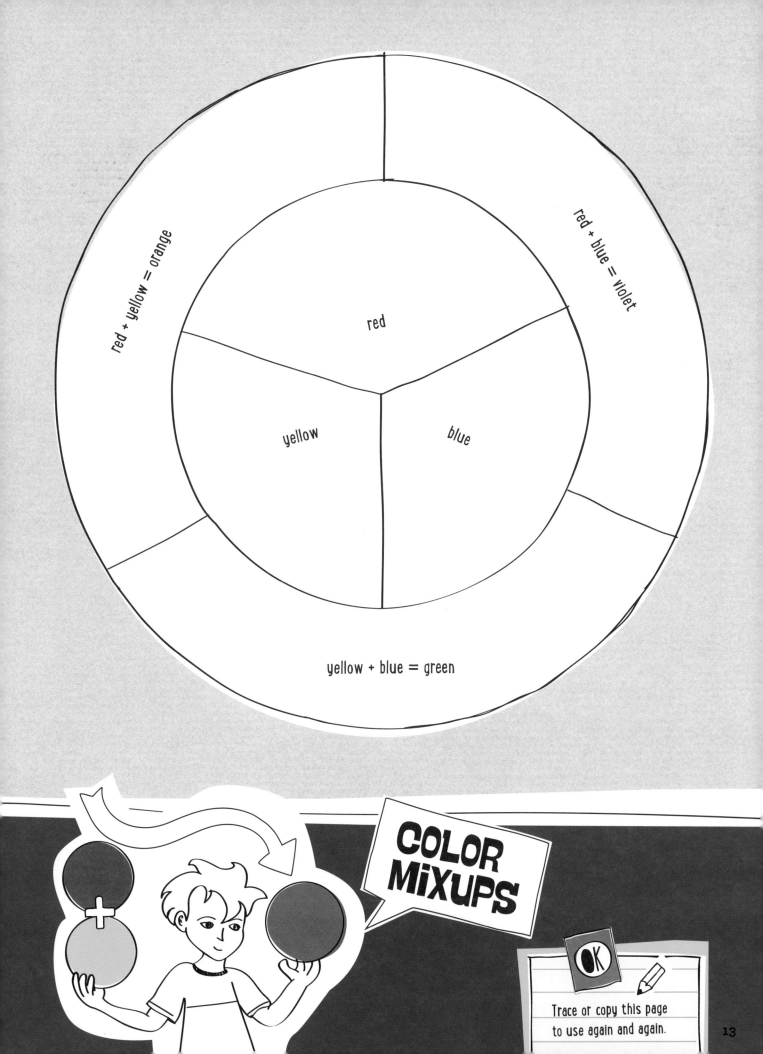

WHY WOULD ANYONE MIX COLORS?

You know that there are paints, markers, crayons, and pencils in so many colors that you can't imagine why anyone would need or want to mix colors.

The best reason to learn how to mix colors is that it helps you understand how color works. And there may be times when you want a certain color and you just don't have it. If you know how to mix colors, you can get any color you want. Besides, it's really fun.

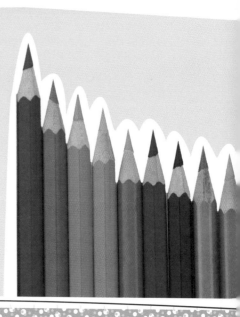

ACTIVITY
Color mixing—Secondary colors

Paint primary and secondary colors on the color wheel from page 13 or the worksheet page called Primary and Secondary Colors.

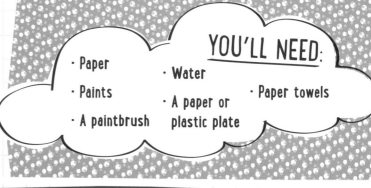

YOU'LL NEED:
- Paper
- Paints
- A paintbrush
- Water
- A paper or plastic plate
- Paper towels

Prepare your paint

Acrylic or poster paint

1. Pour or squeeze a little paint on the edge of a plate. Make sure to spread your colors out: the plate is your **palette**—a place to mix paints.

2. Dip your brush in water and use the brush to pick up a little paint from the plate.

3. Use the space between colors to mix colors.

Watercolors

1. "Wake up" the paints you are going to use by putting a few drops of water on them. For this activity, you'll be using red, blue, and yellow.

2. To use the watercolors, dip your brush in water, rub the wet brush on the paint, and then apply the paint to the paper.

3. When mixing colors, use the lid of the paint box as a **palette**—a place to mix paints.

Paint your color wheel

1. Gather all your materials, including several copies of the blank color wheel from page 13 or the worksheet page called Primary and Secondary Colors. It will probably take several tries for you to get a color wheel that you like.

2. Use blank paper to test the paint colors and to see what they look like when they are dry. (HINT: Paint looks darker when it is wet and lighter when it is dry.)

3. Paint the primary colors in their places on the color wheel. You can probably use the paint just as it is from the watercolor pan, paint tube, or jar.

4. Now for the fun part— MIXING COLORS!

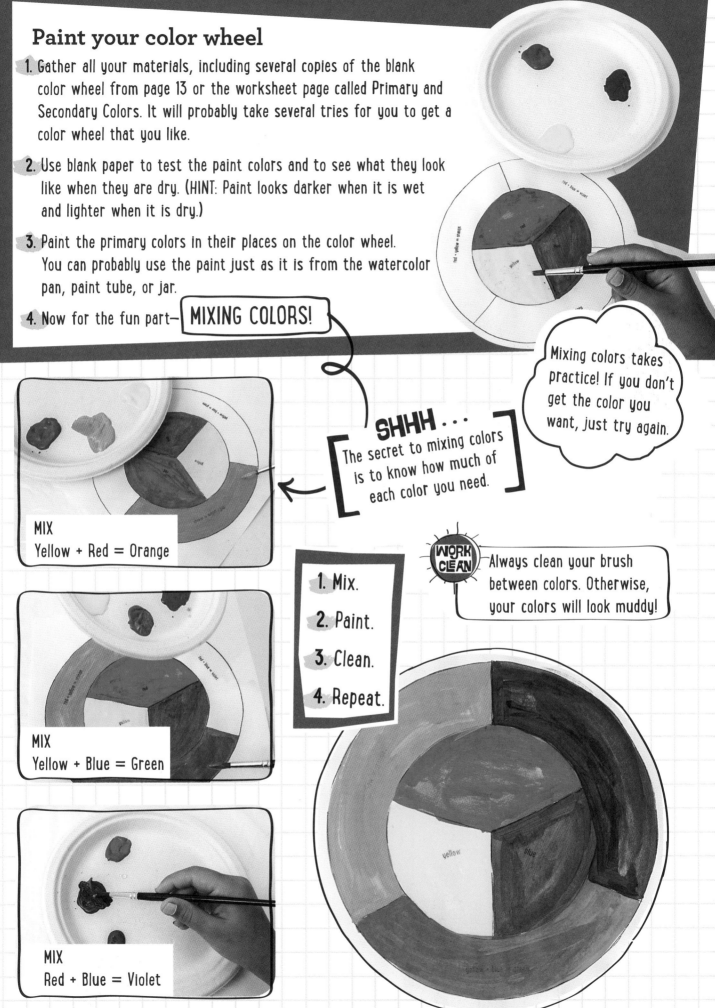

Mixing colors takes practice! If you don't get the color you want, just try again.

SHHH . . .
[The secret to mixing colors is to know how much of each color you need.]

MIX
Yellow + Red = Orange

MIX
Yellow + Blue = Green

MIX
Red + Blue = Violet

1. Mix.
2. Paint.
3. Clean.
4. Repeat.

WORK CLEAN — Always clean your brush between colors. Otherwise, your colors will look muddy!

ACTIVITY
Color blending

Use Sharpie permanent pens and rubbing (isopropyl) alcohol to make Sharpie art.

ask for HELP Be sure to ask permission to use rubbing alcohol.

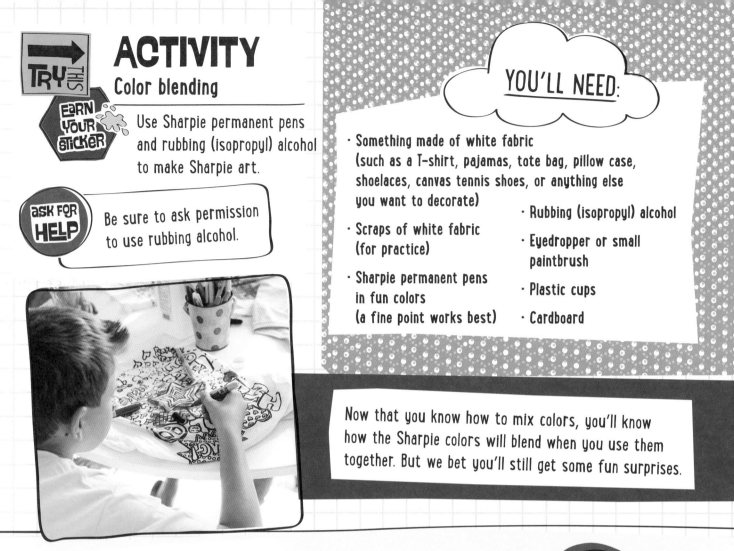

YOU'LL NEED:

- Something made of white fabric (such as a T-shirt, pajamas, tote bag, pillow case, shoelaces, canvas tennis shoes, or anything else you want to decorate)
- Scraps of white fabric (for practice)
- Sharpie permanent pens in fun colors (a fine point works best)
- Rubbing (isopropyl) alcohol
- Eyedropper or small paintbrush
- Plastic cups
- Cardboard

Now that you know how to mix colors, you'll know how the Sharpie colors will blend when you use them together. But we bet you'll still get some fun surprises.

DiD YOU KNOW ...?

>>>>>> This is a good activity to do outside because the Sharpies and alcohol are smelly. If you can't work outside, open a nearby window.

Practice

1. Put some paper or cardboard and plastic on the table underneath your practice scrap of fabric.

2. Draw on the practice scrap with the Sharpies.

3. Slowly drip some of the alcohol on the color, using the eyedropper or small paintbrush. Let it sit for a bit and watch it spread. Keep adding alcohol until you see what it looks like with a lot of alcohol.

Keep your designs simple! Otherwise, everything will blend together too much.

That's a lot!

Now for the real thing

1. Put some paper or cardboard and plastic directly under the fabric you are decorating. For example, if it's a T-shirt, put cardboard inside the shirt so the color doesn't get onto the back of the shirt.

2. Draw or trace a design onto the fabric. Think about what colors you want to use and how they will blend and mix together. You can use lines, dots, shapes—whatever you like.

3. Slowly start to drop some alcohol on the design as you did during your practice. Add more as you like.

4. Watch the colors spread and blend. Remember, don't put on too much alcohol or your design will just blend away.

ASK FOR HELP Heat set the colors by putting your project into a hot dryer for 10-20 minutes.

HERE'S AN IDEA!

If you are using circular designs, put the fabric over a cup and hold it with a rubber band. This will help keep the design in a circle.

Hi, Michael! We like your backpack!

When Audrey's done, she's gonna rock that bandana!

17

HAVE A COLOR WHEEL PARTY!

Have everyone help make a giant torn-paper color wheel—like the one you made on page 12, only much bigger!

Color wheel bean bag game

SET UP

1. Make primary-color bean bags by gluing together the edges of 2 pieces of felt to make pouches. Leave a small hole along the edge of each pouch. Fill the bag with beans through the hole, then glue the hole up.

2. Use chalk to draw a big color wheel outside, using the picture (at right) as an example. Draw 3 starting lines around the wheel.

START THE GAME

1. All players pick a primary color.

2. Stand at the starting line and aim for your color.

If your bean bag lands in <u>your</u> primary color, you get **100** points! If your bean bag lands in one of your secondary colors, you get **50** points! If your bean bag lands in a different color, you get **0** points.

EXAMPLE: If your bean bags are red, you get **100** points for landing in red, **50** points for landing in violet or orange, and **0** points for landing in blue, green, or yellow.

ASK FOR HELP A little food coloring goes a long way. Always start with just a drop and add more as needed.

Put your color mixing skills to work!

Pour water into an ice cube tray, then add different colors of food coloring to each cube. After the ice cubes are frozen, combine them in glasses and watch the colors blend as they melt. Guess what color the water will be when they are all melted.

Make color wheel cupcakes and a colorful fruit or veggie tray.

TERTIARY

pronounced (tur-shee-err-ree)

Let's add more colors!
Now that you know all about primary and secondary colors, there's one more group of colors to get acquainted with. They are called **tertiary** colors, or **tertiaries**, and they are the colors that you get when you mix a primary color with the secondary color that is next to it on the color wheel.

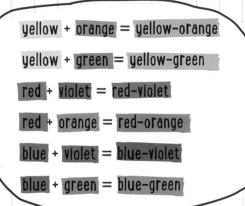

ACTIVITY
Color mixing—Tertiary colors
Paint primary, secondary, and tertiary colors using the color wheel from the next page or the worksheet page called Tertiary Colors.

YOU'LL NEED:
- Paper
- Paints
- A paintbrush
- Water
- A paper or plastic plate
- Paper towels

1. Gather all your materials, including several copies of the blank color wheel. It will probably take several tries for you to get a color wheel that you like.

2. Start by filling in the primary colors (red, yellow, and blue).

3. Mix the secondary colors. Start with yellow and red to make orange. Mix some extra so you can use it when you mix the tertiary colors in Step 5.

4. Mix yellow and blue to make green. Mix blue and red to make violet. Be sure to mix enough of each to use in the next step.

5. Use the same process to mix the 6 tertiary colors and paint them on your color wheel.

REMINDER
WORK CLEAN — Always clean your brush between colors. Otherwise, your colors will look muddy!

yellow + orange = yellow-orange

yellow + green = yellow-green

red + violet = red-violet

red + orange = red-orange

blue + violet = blue-violet

blue + green = blue-green

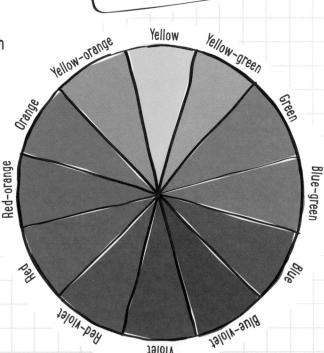

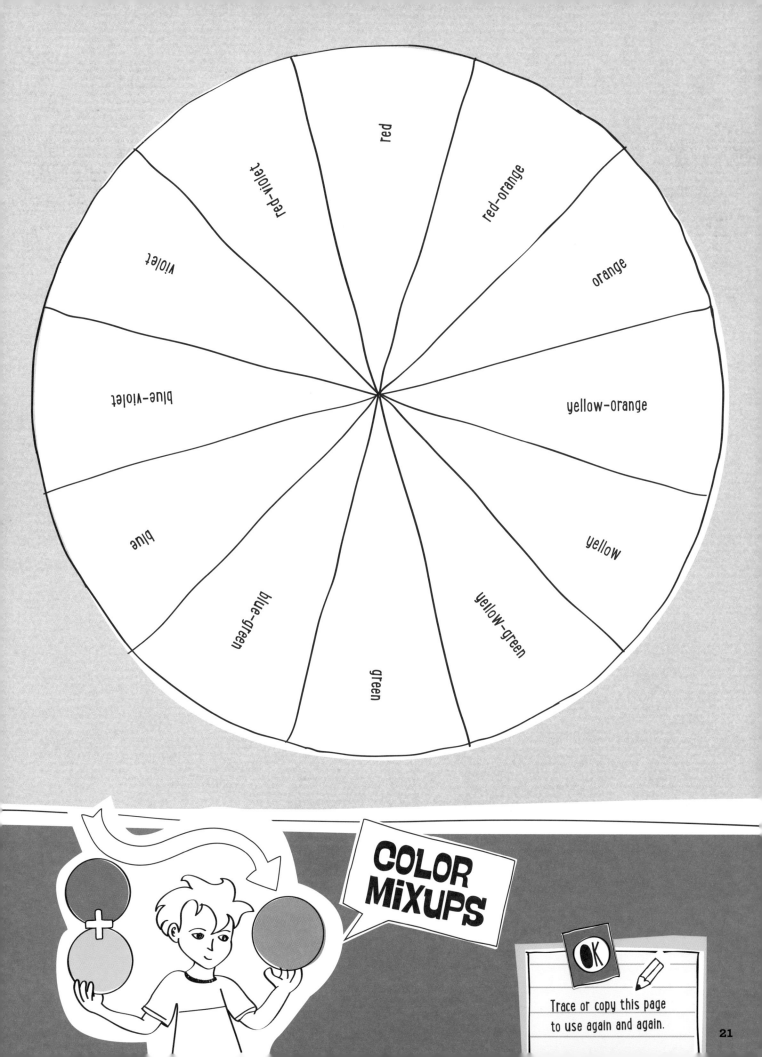

COLOR MiXUPS

OK
Trace or copy this page
to use again and again.

Tints, tones, and shades

In addition to all the colors you've seen so far, all the colors on the color wheel have <u>tints</u>, <u>tones</u>, and <u>shades</u>.

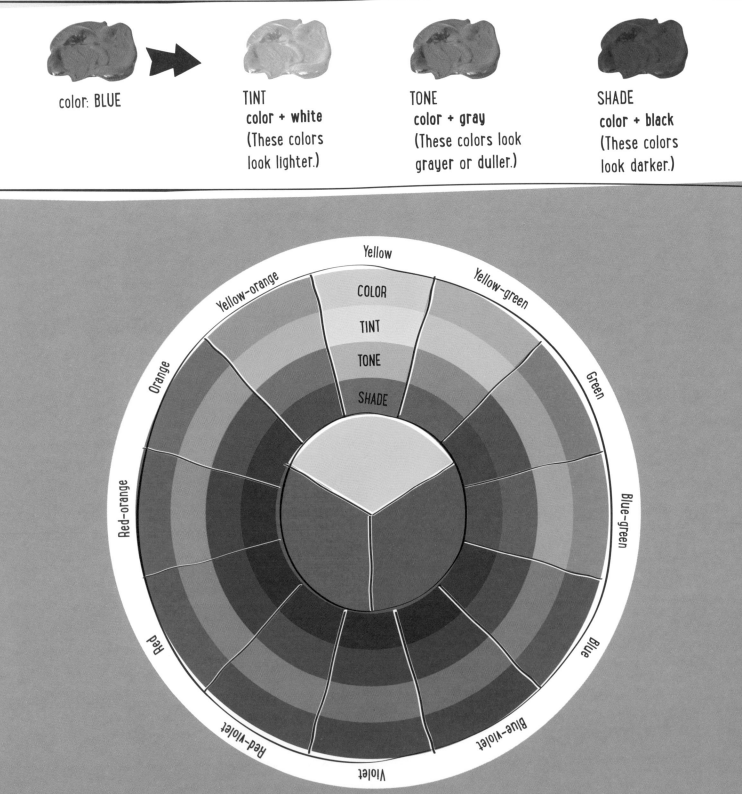

color: BLUE

TINT
color + white
(These colors look lighter.)

TONE
color + gray
(These colors look grayer or duller.)

SHADE
color + black
(These colors look darker.)

ACTIVITY

→ TRY THIS

EARN YOUR STICKER

Mix tints, tones, and shades

Mix your own tints, tones, and shades.

YOU'LL NEED:
- Acrylic or fabric paints
- A paintbrush
- Water
- Paper towels

1. To mix a tint, start with white paint and add your color bit by bit.

2. To mix a tone, start with your color paint and add gray bit by bit.

3. To mix a shade, start with your color paint and add black bit by bit.

Color   Tint   Tone   Shade

White + Black = Gray

- Fill in the boxes as you make your own tints, tones, and shades.

- Use the same color for all 3 so you can see the differences.

- If you don't have gray paint, mix just a little bit of black into some white to make gray.

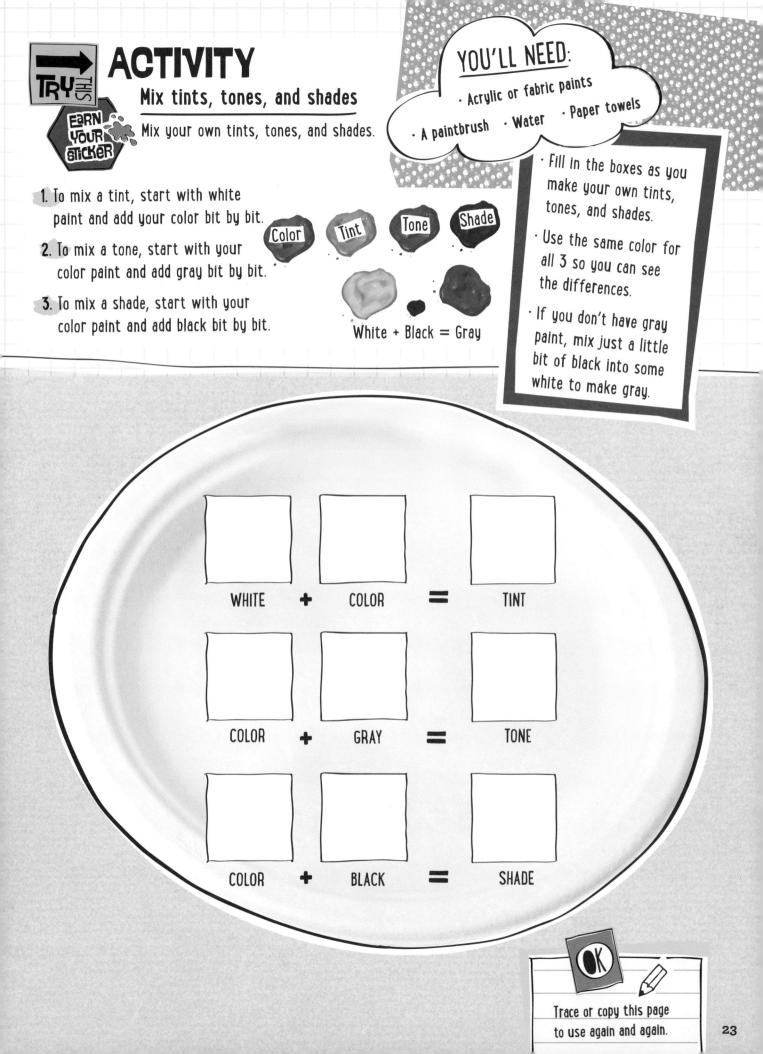

WHITE +	COLOR =	TINT
COLOR +	GRAY =	TONE
COLOR +	BLACK =	SHADE

OK

Trace or copy this page to use again and again.

COLOR JOKES

Try these on your friends!

Q: What would you call the USA if everyone had a pink car?
A: A pink carnation.

Q: What do you do with a green monster?
A: Wait until she's ripe.

Q: What's orange and sounds like a parrot?
A: A carrot!

Q: Why did the tomato turn red?
A: Because it saw the salad dressing.

Q: What color socks do bears wear?
A: They don't wear socks; they have bear feet.

Q: What is a cat's favorite color?
A: PURR-PLE

Q: What bird is always sad?
A: The blue jay.

Q: What do you do when you find a blue elephant?
A: Cheer her up.

Q: What did the ivy say to the grass?
A: I'm green with envy because you are greener.

Q: What is a cheerleader's favorite color?
A: YELLER!
>>>

Q: What's gray and blue and very big?
A: An elephant holding its breath.

Q: What color is a burp?
A: Burple.

ACTIVITY

Using tints, tones, and shades on fabric

Use paint on fabric to create a blended look.

SHADE   COLOR   TINT

SHADE

TINT

COLOR:
Red-violet

YOU'LL NEED:

- Plain white fabric:
  Pieces about 5″ × 20″
  Scraps in many sizes

- Acrylic or fabric paints

- A paintbrush

- Water

- 3 small plastic containers

- Plastic to cover the table

- Paper towels

IDEA!

You can also use light-colored fabric that you have around the house.

Prepare your paints

1. Thick paint is hard to spread on fabric, so you'll probably want to slightly thin your paints with water. Pour about ¼ cup of paint into the first container. Add water ½ teaspoon at a time to the paint. Every time you add water, mix the paint and then test it on a damp scrap to see if you can spread it easily.

2. Put about 2 tablespoons of white paint in the second container. Thin the white paint as you thinned your main color.

3. Add about ¼ teaspoon of your thinned color to the white paint and mix well.

4. Pour half of your thinned main color into the third container. Add black or gray to the third container to make a tone or shade.

5. Be sure there is a noticeable difference between the 3 containers of paint.

Start painting

1. Get the fabric wet. Squeeze it out.

2. Start in the middle of your fabric and paint the main color.

3. Switch to the tint on one side.

4. Paint the tone or shade on the other side.

Work quickly so the paint doesn't dry.

5. Use your hands or a clean, wet paintbrush to blend the paint where the colors meet. You can also spray on a little water to help the colors blend.

6. Let the paint dry.

You've just created an **ombré** piece of fabric, which means the colors blend into one another.

pronounced (om-bray)

TRY THESE! >>>>>

Tear your ombré piece of fabric into strips 1/4″–1 1/2″ wide, depending on what you are making.

Shoelaces

Tear fabric into strips about 1″ wide then lace into shoes. For fun, attach a safety pin with colorful beads.

Sandals

1. Stitch down the center of the strip.

2. Gather the strips by pushing the fabric together. Knot the thread when you are done.

3. Glue the fabric to your flip-flops or sandals.

Bracelet

1. Attach a button to 1 end of 3 strips.

2. Braid.

3. Make a slit along each strip on the other end. Slide the button through the slits to secure your bracelet.

How to Braid

1. A over B

2. C over A

HINT:
The strand that is not crossed goes over the middle.

3. B over C

REMEMBER:
"Pull" up to create the braid.

Headband

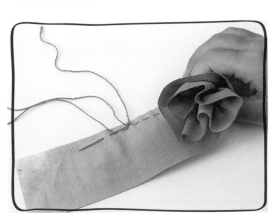

1. Tear a strip of fabric about 1½˝ wide.

2. Sew a straight stitch along the edge of the fabric strip.

3. Pull the thread to gather the fabric and roll it up as you go to make the flower. Knot the thread when you are done rolling.

4. Glue the flower to a headband. Tear 2 strips about ³/₄˝ wide from your ombré piece of fabric and wrap them around the headband to cover it. Cover the end of the flower, too.

27

Value

There's one more important thing to know about color: Every color has a **value**.

Value means how light or dark a color is.

Value can be a little tricky because the value of a color depends on the colors and values around it.

To get started, think about value as light, medium, and dark.

What value is this color?

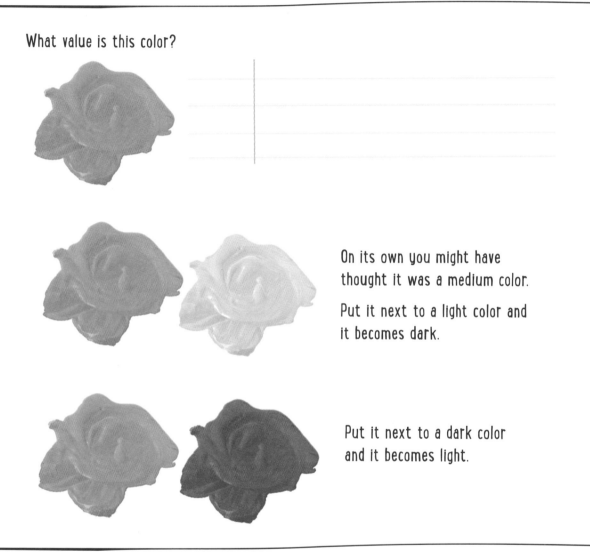

On its own you might have thought it was a medium color.

Put it next to a light color and it becomes dark.

Put it next to a dark color and it becomes light.

THINK aBOUT it

TINTS (a color + white) are **LIGHT VALUES**.

TONES (a color + gray) are **MEDIUM VALUES**.

SHADES (a color + black) are **DARK VALUES**.

Design in black and white

Why does value matter?

When thinking about value, it doesn't matter if you are drawing a picture or painting a wall. If all the colors in the design have the same value, the different shapes in the design blend together.

But if you have light values and dark values, you can make a design really stand out.

And using value, you can make the design look different depending on where you put the light, medium, and dark values.

These are the same fabric designs, using light, medium, and dark values.

Design using light and medium values

Cute headband! Did you notice that the flowers have different values of the same color?

Design using medium and dark values

ACTIVITY

How can you use value?

Color the designs on the next page using value.

This design uses dark and light values to create an optical illusion. See how the spider web looks like it is moving in and out?

1. Copy the designs on the next page 2 or 3 times. Make more copies if you need them.

2. Use markers, colored pencils, or paints to fill in each design several times. Change the placement of the light, medium, and dark values.

3. See how many different combinations you can come up with for each design.

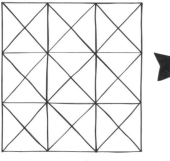

DESIGN 1

If you use the same value, the design does not stand out.

If you use light and dark values, the design stands out.

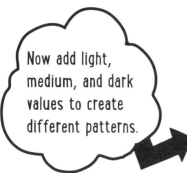

Now add light, medium, and dark values to create different patterns.

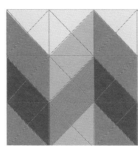

Look closely and you can see that all three of these use the same basic design, but the different colors and values make the patterns different. Pretty cool!

DID YOU KNOW ...?

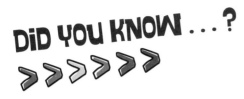

If you are using paints, make lighter values by adding water or white to the paint; make darker values by adding a bit of black to the paint. If you are using markers or pencils, press harder for the dark values and don't press down very hard for the light values. You can also use white, gray, and black crayons or pencils to change a color's value.

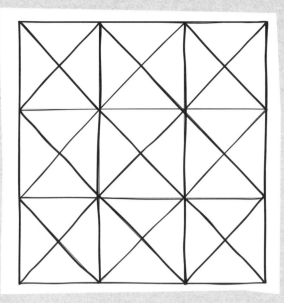

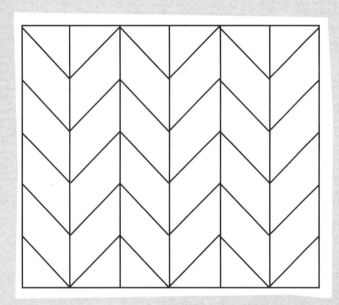

NOW THAT'S a GOOD VALUE.

Trace or copy this page
to use again and again.

Using color

Now that you know some things about color and the color wheel, let's see how you can use the color wheel.

The color wheel is a great tool to turn to when you're not sure what colors to use. The most common way to use it is to look at standard <u>color plans</u> (sometimes called color schemes or color relationships).

> Wearing clothes in a monochromatic color plan is an easy way to make sure everything you are wearing goes together.

Color plans

Here are some commonly used color plans, or color schemes.

<u>Monochromatic</u> means "one color." If you're using just one color, you'll want to use the color's tints, tones, and shades (page 22)—otherwise, it's **really** boring.

<u>Analogous</u> colors are next to each other on the color wheel.

<u>Complementary</u> colors are across from each other on the color wheel.

Monochromatic

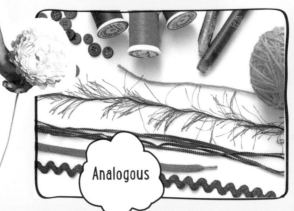
Analogous

Complementary

MONOCHROMATIC

ACTIVITY

Using a monochromatic color scheme

Go to your closet or dresser and pick out a set of clothes in monochromatic colors—or color in Roy G. BV to give him a monochromatic look.

Trace or copy this page to use again and again.

ACTIVITY
Make tissue paper flowers

Choose a monochromatic color scheme to make flowers.

1. Pick out 3 sheets of tissue paper in a monochromatic color scheme.

2. Cut out 4 squares 5″ × 5″ of each color.

TiP
Use a ruler to draw cutting lines for your squares.

3. Layer 4 squares at a time, fold them, and cut the end in a petal shape.

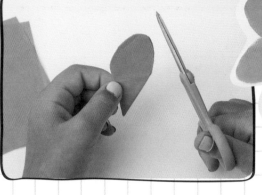

4. Gently push each layer of tissue paper onto a chenille stem. Start with the darkest color and work your way to the lightest color.

5. When all the layers are on the chenille stem, bend the end of the chenille stem to form the center of the flower and to keep the tissue paper from coming off. Bend the chenille stem at the base of the flower to keep the flower in place.

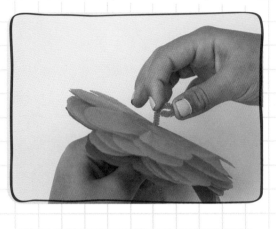

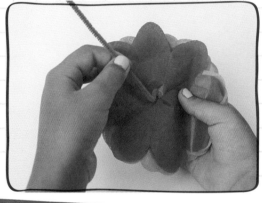

6. One layer at a time, gently crumple the layers of tissue paper.

TRY THESE! >>>>>>>

Make these flowers in many sizes by using bigger or smaller squares.

Make the different parts of the flower different sizes. Start with smaller squares for the flower center and make the squares bigger for the outside parts of the flower.

Make a whole bouquet of flowers.

Turn a flower into a ring or a pin.

COOL
Calm and soothing

WARM
Bright and energetic

WARM AND COOL COLORS

Warm and cool colors are special kinds of analogous colors. The warm colors are on one side of the color wheel and the cool colors are on the other side of the color wheel.

ANALOGOUS

Even three can be friends . . .

Analogous colors are next to each other on the color wheel. They always play well together and are nice to look at. All of a color's tints, tones, and shades can be included in an analogous color scheme.

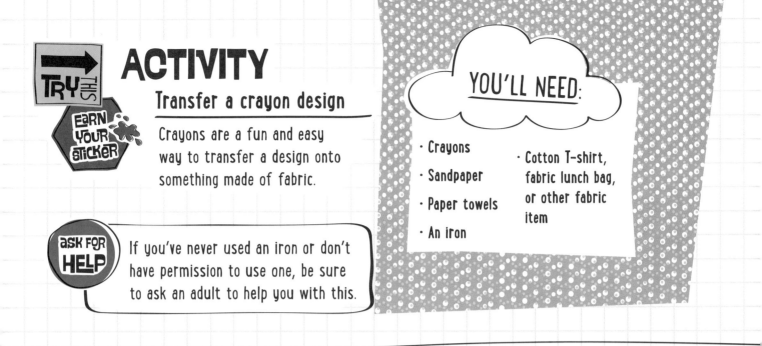

ACTIVITY
Transfer a crayon design

Crayons are a fun and easy way to transfer a design onto something made of fabric.

TRY THIS

EARN YOUR STICKER

ask for HELP If you've never used an iron or don't have permission to use one, be sure to ask an adult to help you with this.

YOU'LL NEED:

- Crayons
- Sandpaper
- Paper towels
- An iron
- Cotton T-shirt, fabric lunch bag, or other fabric item

DiD YOU KNOW...? >>>>>>

Sandpaper comes in different grits—which means how rough or smooth the surface is. The rougher the grit, the more bumpy-looking the design will be when you transfer it. Try different grits to see what you like best.

1. Draw your design onto a piece of sandpaper. Press hard with the crayon so lots of color gets onto the sandpaper.

2. Turn on the iron to the highest setting. If your iron has a steam setting, turn it off.

3. Place the sandpaper with the color side down on the fabric you're transferring to. Peek underneath to make sure the design will be where you want it.

4. Place a piece of paper towel on top of the sandpaper.

5. Iron firmly for about 30 seconds. Don't move the sandpaper, but peek underneath a corner to see how the transfer is going. If you need to transfer more color, keep ironing.

6. Remove the sandpaper and place a clean paper towel on top of the transferred design. Iron to remove excess crayon. Do this a few times, until no more crayon comes off on the paper towel.

7. When it's time to wash the item, turn it inside out (if possible) and wash in cold water.

IMPORTANT

Anything you draw on the sandpaper will appear in reverse when it's transferred. If you are using words or letters, you'll need to write them backward.

MORE FUN DESIGNS

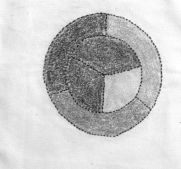

COMPLEMENTARY

○ ○ ○ ○ ○ ○ ○ ○ ○ ○ ○

Complementary colors are across from each other on the color wheel. When you want colors that are exciting and lively together, use complementary colors. You can even use pairs of complementary colors. All of a color's tints, tones, and shades can be included in a complementary color scheme.

Yellow
Yellow-orange
Yellow-green
Orange
Green
Red-orange
Blue-green
Red
Blue
Red-violet
Blue-violet
Violet

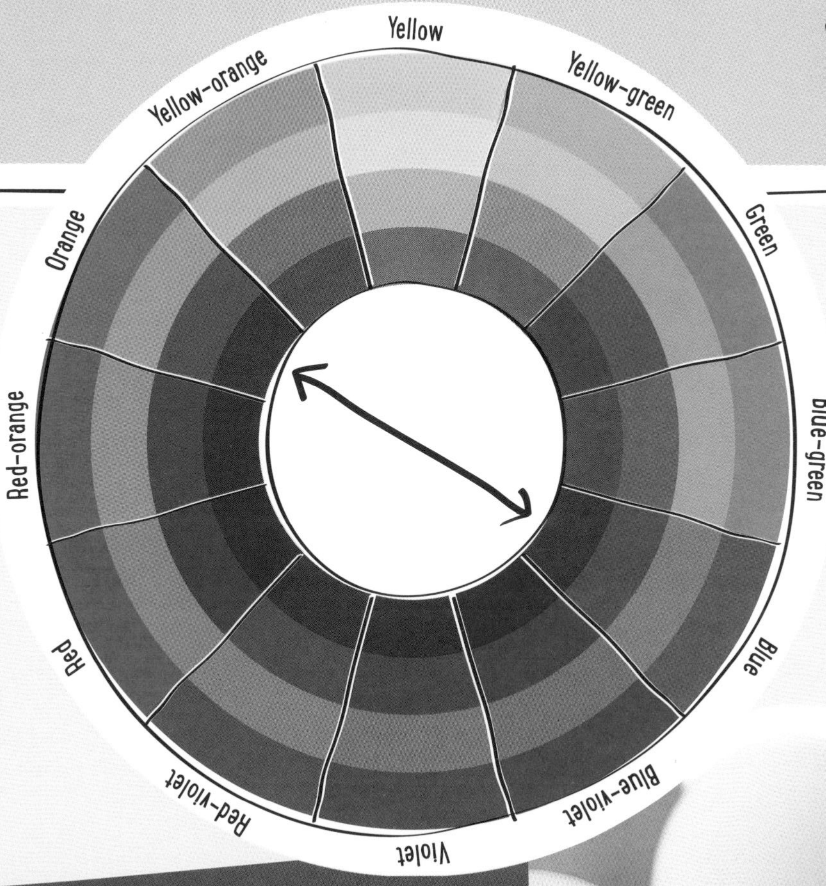

Sophie's canary-yellow sunglasses are the perfect complement to her lavender dress. Her blue-green balloons complement her red-orange ones, too!

KNOW YOUR SPELLING

By the way, note the spelling: You can compl(i)ment your friend on her use of a compl(e)mentary color scheme.

39

ACTIVITY

*Mixing complementary colors

Fill in the boxes on the next page with complementary colors.

YOU'LL NEED:

- Paper
- Paints
- A paintbrush
- Water
- Paper
- Paper towels

The only way to know what complementary colors will look like when mixed together is to try it with the paints that you have. Look at the color wheel to the left or use the color wheel poster to try out different combinations of complementary colors to see what you get. We'll give you a few combinations to get you started; then you can experiment.

What happens when you mix together complementary colors?

We're glad you asked.

When you mix together complementary colors, you get what is called a "neutral" color. Some of the neutrals are pretty, and some look ... well, to be honest, they look like mud. This is why when you mix some colors together your mix sometimes looks muddy.

Red   +   Green   =   Mud

40

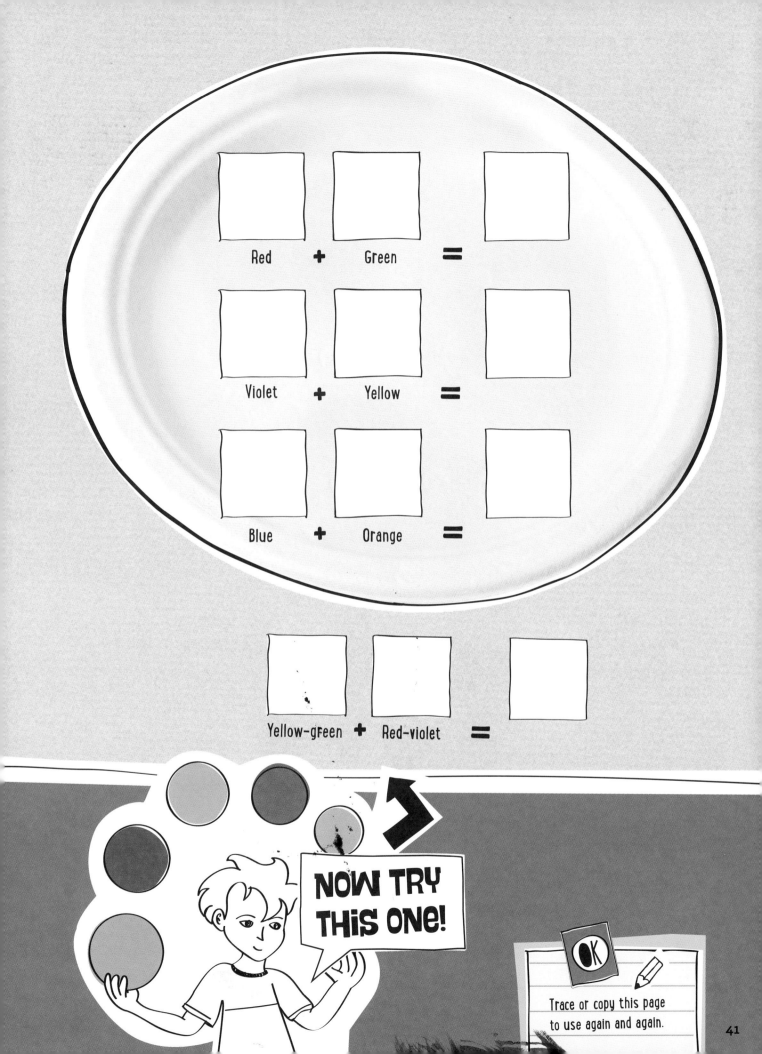

Red + Green =

Violet + Yellow =

Blue + Orange =

Yellow-green + Red-violet =

NOW TRY THIS ONE!

OK
Trace or copy this page to use again and again.

ACTIVITY

Quick color quiz

Pick the answer that is MOST right, based on what you've learned in this book.
(Answers are on page 62.)

COLOR QUIZ

Red and green are:
- ○ Christmas colors
- ○ complementary colors
- ○ primary colors

A color + white is:
- ○ a tint
- ○ an Easter color
- ○ a tertiary color

Red, orange, and yellow are:
- ○ primary colors
- ○ warm colors
- ○ analogous colors

Yellow and violet are:
- ○ pretty together
- ○ cool colors
- ○ complementary colors

Dark green, green, and light green are:
- ○ monochromatic
- ○ dramatic
- ○ diplomatic

A color + black is:
- ○ a dark color
- ○ a shade
- ○ boring

Green, yellow-green, and yellow are:
- ○ analogous colors
- ○ analog colors
- ○ aromatic colors

Red-violet and yellow-green are:
- ○ bright colors
- ○ hyphenated colors
- ○ tertiary colors

Green, blue-green, and blue are:
- ○ complementary colors
- ○ analogous colors
- ○ cool colors

A color + gray is:
- ○ a hint
- ○ a tone
- ○ a tertiary color

If you got 6-10 answers right, give yourself a sticker on your Certificate of COLOR-ology.

If you got 1-5 answers right, read up and try again!

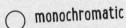

Trace or copy this page to use again and again.

ACTIVITY
Spin art

Spin paints together. Your choice of color scheme.

TRY THIS
EARN YOUR STICKER

TiP >>>>>>

If you don't have a spin art machine, ask if there is an old salad spinner in the house that you can use. If you don't have one, you can probably find one at a thrift store.

WORK CLEAN

Pick a **few** colors to use. Think about your color schemes. If you use too many colors, the result will look muddy.

We're using blue-green, violet, and blue.

1. You're going to be dripping the paint, so you want it thin enough to drip nicely. Add water as needed, but don't thin it too much because you want the colors to be strong.

2. Cut the paper or paper plates to fit the spin art machine or the salad spinner. You may need to tape the plate down to keep it from moving around too much.

3. Start the machine or salad spinner spinning. If you are using a salad spinner, start spinning and then take off the lid.

4. Squeeze out some paint or use the paintbrush to drop thin paint onto the spinning paper and watch the colors blend.

TRY THESE! >>>>>>

Ideas for your spin art

Card

Frame your original artwork in a card.

T-shirt

To put spin art on a T-shirt, follow these steps:

1. Place blank paper circle in spinner, then spray with water.

2. Create your spin art with acrylic or **fabric paint** (a special kind of acrylic paint made especially to use on fabric).

3. Spray a little bit more water on your art.

4. Flip your art onto a T-shirt and rub hard to transfer the paint!

IMPORTANT: Work quickly so the paint doesn't dry before you get it on the T-shirt.

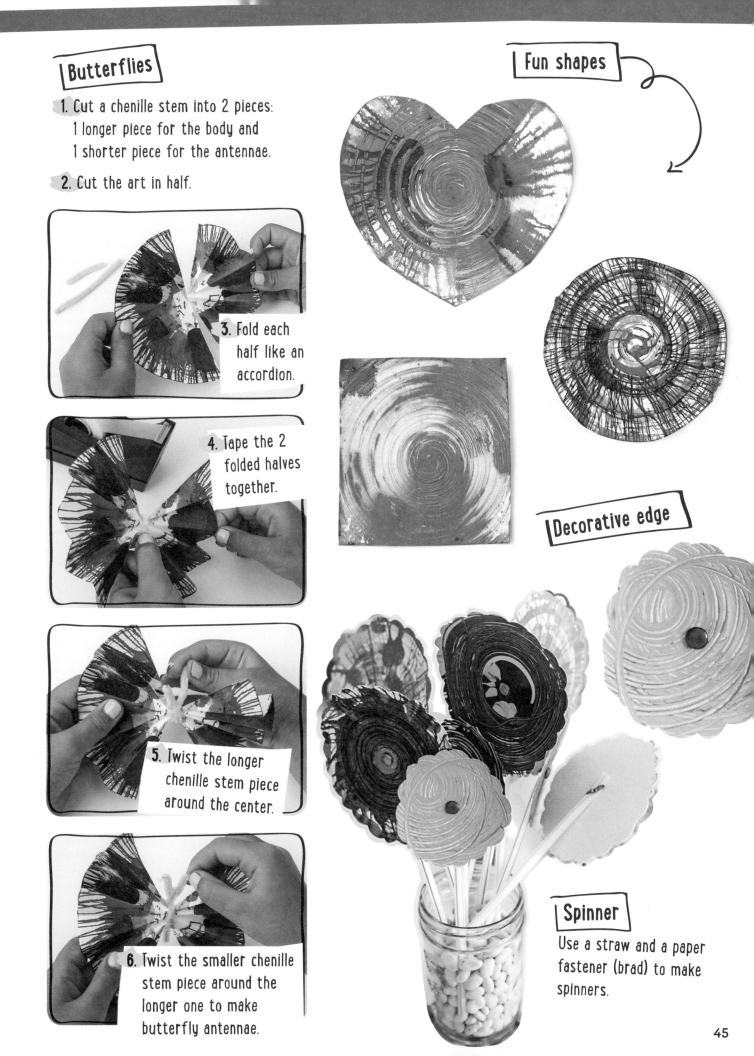

Butterflies

1. Cut a chenille stem into 2 pieces:
   1 longer piece for the body and
   1 shorter piece for the antennae.

2. Cut the art in half.

3. Fold each half like an accordion.

4. Tape the 2 folded halves together.

5. Twist the longer chenille stem piece around the center.

6. Twist the smaller chenille stem piece around the longer one to make butterfly antennae.

Fun shapes

Decorative edge

Spinner

Use a straw and a paper fastener (brad) to make spinners.

45

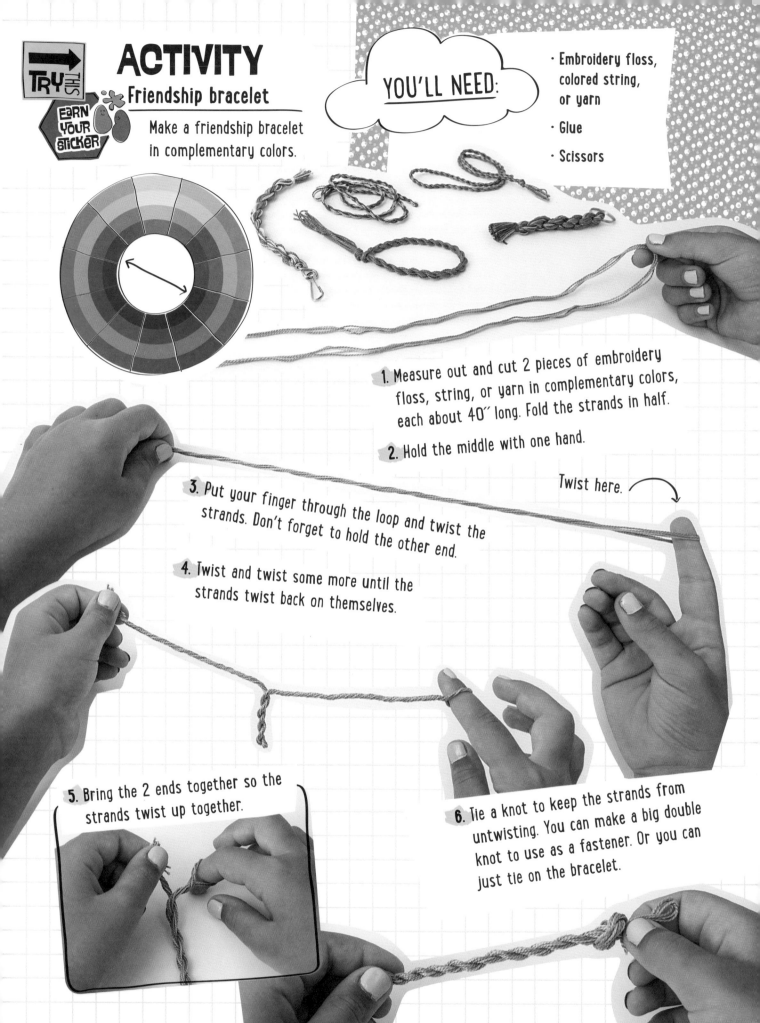

ACTIVITY
Friendship bracelet

Make a friendship bracelet in complementary colors.

YOU'LL NEED:

- Embroidery floss, colored string, or yarn
- Glue
- Scissors

1. Measure out and cut 2 pieces of embroidery floss, string, or yarn in complementary colors, each about 40˝ long. Fold the strands in half.

2. Hold the middle with one hand.

Twist here.

3. Put your finger through the loop and twist the strands. Don't forget to hold the other end.

4. Twist and twist some more until the strands twist back on themselves.

5. Bring the 2 ends together so the strands twist up together.

6. Tie a knot to keep the strands from untwisting. You can make a big double knot to use as a fastener. Or you can just tie on the bracelet.

This is a fun activity to do at a party or with a friend.

TRY THESE! >>>>>

- For thicker bracelets or to use as a key lanyard, use more strands or thicker strands.

- Use pairs of complementary colors or use tints, tones, and shades of the colors.

- To make one longer to wear as a necklace, start with strands about 54″ long.

- Make a bunch and wear them together.

Have a COLORFUL week

Primary SUNDAY
Find pictures of sports teams whose uniforms are primary colors (red, yellow, or blue).

Monochromatic MONDAY
Wear your monochromatic braided bracelet (page 27) or find things in your house that are monochromatic.

Tertiary TUESDAY
Wear a tertiary color (yellow-orange, yellow-green, red-violet, red-orange, blue-violet, or blue-green).

Complementary WEDNESDAY
When you see someone wearing complementary colors, give the person a compliment.

Analogous THURSDAY
Draw a picture using analogous colors.

Free-for-All FRIDAY
Just be colorful!

Secondary SATURDAY
Make sure you include something that is a secondary color (orange, green, or violet) for breakfast, lunch, and dinner.

How artists use color

Here's a chance for you to see how color is used by people who use it all the time. The fabric designs on this page are the exact same pattern as this.

Valori Wells, a fabric designer, made each of these designs look different by using different colors and values.

Let's take a look at them.

Use the color wheel to answer the questions. Answers are on page 62.

1. Which <u>analogous</u> colors are used?

2. Which <u>complementary</u> colors are used?

3. Can you name the <u>complementary</u> colors and the <u>analogous</u> colors in this pattern?

TRY THIS

EARN YOUR STICKER

ACTIVITY
Write color haiku

pronounced (hy-koo)

Haiku are short poems that usually express a feeling. Haiku were originally developed by Japanese poets but are now written in many languages all over the world.

HaiKu

>>> Ve-ry bright yel-low
It makes me feel so sun-ny
Hap-py hap-py day

Now it's your turn!
See what you can write.

Haiku are usually 17 syllables:

· 5 syllables in the first line

· 7 syllables in the second line

· 5 syllables in the third line

So ma-ny co-lors
Blue is my fa-vor-ite one
Like the sky and sea

A COLOR HAIKU

OK

Trace or copy this page to use again and again.

How colors affect each other

Remember back on page 28, where you saw how the value (lightness or darkness) of a color depends on what other colors are around it?

Well ... there are more ways that colors affect each other.

COOL

WARM

>>>>>>>

LOOK AT THIS

Notice how the warmer colors look like they are coming to the front and the cooler colors look like they are moving to the back.

A warm color can make another color look cooler.

A cool color can make another color look warmer.

Complementary colors are exciting together.

Analogous colors are calmer together.

YOU'LL NEED:
· Markers, colored pencils, paint supplies, or crayons

OK

Trace or copy this page to use again and again.

TRY THIS

EARN YOUR STICKER

COOL

ACTIVITY
How colors affect each other

Use markers, colored pencils, paint, or crayons on the star above. Make up your own color combinations and see how the colors affect each other.

How colors affect you

Whether you know it or not, colors have meanings based on how people react to them and use them.

STOP

Red is bright and bold. It gets your attention, so it is often used as a warning (STOP sign). It is also the color of a hot fire and of love (red hearts).

Seeing red—to be angry

Turn red—to be embarrassed

Red-letter day—a very important occasion

Caught red-handed—caught doing something wrong

Red carpet—a welcome for someone important

Did you know red means good luck in China?

Orange is associated with joy, energy, enthusiasm, creativity, and happiness. It is also one of the colors of the fall and harvest (pumpkins and orange leaves).

Q: What's your favorite fruit?
A: Oranges, because they have appeal.

Yellow is the brightest color; it makes us feel happy and energetic (bright sunny days).

Because yellow is so bright, traffic warning signs are often yellow.

Did you know 75% of the pencils in the United States are yellow?

Green is the color of nature, growth, harmony, safety, freshness, and calmness. Green is also commonly associated with money.

Greenhorn—to be new at something; to be a beginner

Green—to be envious, or green with envy

Green-Eyed Monster—jealousy

Get the green light—to get the go-ahead

Have a green thumb—to be a good gardener

green light GO
red light STOP

I'm going green—becoming environmentally conscious.

Greenback—money

Blue is the color of the sky and the water. It expresses calmness, trust, loyalty, wisdom, and confidence.

Expressions that include blue have many different meanings.

Feeling blue—to feel sad

Out of the blue—suddenly

True blue—to be faithful

Wild blue yonder—up in the sky; a faraway place

Blue ribbon—first place, the best quality

Violet (purple) has historically been a color for royalty. A long time ago, it was very, very expensive to dye fabric purple, so only very rich kings and queens could wear purple fabric. Purple is often associated with wisdom, dignity, independence, creativity, mystery, and magic.

Purple prose—flowery romantic writing

Purple heart—a medal awarded to a U.S. soldier wounded in battle

ACTIVITY

What colors/season are you?

Pick one—there's no wrong or right answer. Find out what colors/season you are.

If you picked mostly A's, you are **spring** (orange, yellow-orange, yellow)—you are enthusiastic, creative, and friendly.

If you picked mostly B's, you are **summer** (yellow-green, green, blue-green)—you are outgoing and love to have fun.

If you picked mostly C's, you are **fall** (red-orange, red, red-violet)—you are energetic and responsible.

If you picked mostly D's, you are **winter** (violet, blue-violet, blue)—you are reserved, loyal, and trustworthy.

If you could live anywhere, what would you live near?

- ○ A) A big park
- ○ B) The beach
- ○ C) The woods
- ○ D) The mountains

You are:

- ○ A) Friendly to everyone
- ○ B) Loud and chatty
- ○ C) Always ready to take on a new project
- ○ D) Quiet and smart

What kind of weather do you like best?

- ○ A) Rainy
- ○ B) Hot and sunny
- ○ C) Dry and cloudy
- ○ D) Cold and sunny

If you had a free day, what would you want to do?

- ○ A) Play with friends
- ○ B) Go to an amusement park
- ○ C) Go for a walk
- ○ D) Read a book

You prefer:

- ○ A) Soft light colors (tints)
- ○ B) Bright, bold colors (pure colors)
- ○ C) Soft dark colors (tones)
- ○ D) Deep dark colors (shades)

What type of car do you like?

- ○ A) VW Bug
- ○ B) Ferrari
- ○ C) Prius
- ○ D) BMW

What's your favorite food?

- ○ A) Hot wings
- ○ B) Sushi
- ○ C) Fruit
- ○ D) Broccoli

What's your favorite drink?

- ○ A) Bubble tea
- ○ B) Fruit smoothie
- ○ C) Hot tea
- ○ D) Milk

Trace or copy this page to use again and again.

ACTIVITY
Word find

Find the words below.
They can be forward, backward, or diagonal.

CONGRATULATIONS

If you found at least 12 words,
give yourself a sticker on your
Certificate of COLOR-ology when
you are finished.

If you didn't find at least
12 words, keep trying!

Answers on page 62.

D	A	D	A	K	S	F	K	S	R	P	P	A	T	W
F	B	D	D	X	D	S	D	W	T	H	R	S	A	E
H	L	C	K	O	E	D	A	H	S	J	I	R	H	R
U	U	J	G	M	F	O	R	A	U	S	M	D	Z	G
M	E	R	B	G	F	P	C	G	O	D	A	F	D	D
S	O	W	K	H	N	Y	D	H	I	W	R	I	F	G
G	V	A	S	E	C	O	N	D	A	R	Y	T	V	J
P	T	O	N	E	D	R	G	L	D	C	T	D	I	K
L	E	I	U	A	M	C	O	L	O	R	R	G	O	L
E	Q	A	N	U	D	X	H	O	R	S	G	T	L	G
Z	K	K	T	T	Z	A	J	O	R	A	N	G	E	B
Y	E	L	L	O	W	W	A	C	T	R	E	H	T	O
V	L	K	T	W	X	F	W	I	H	G	W	D	G	U
D	C	N	E	E	R	G	M	L	J	B	D	J	E	E
U	K	O	W	P	A	Y	C	F	M	X	C	W	U	R

Blue	Orange	Shade	Warm
Color	Primary	Tint	Yellow
Cool	Red	Tone	
Green	Secondary	Violet	

Trace or copy this page
to use again and again.

55

ASK ROY G. BV

We've asked our color specialist Roy G. BV to help us answer some of your color questions.

Q: I have this light pink bedspread my parents won't let me get rid of. What can I do so my room doesn't look so babyish?

BEFORE

AFTER

A: How about updating your room with some new accessories, such as a lamp, pennant flags, and pillow case? Pink is a tint of red, so bringing in some green (the complement of red) accents will give it some zing. Remember that you can use all the tints, tones, and shades of green. Add in some of green's analogous buddies (yellow-green and blue-green), and I'll bet you can find a winning combo.

Memo Board

1. Cut foam core to the size board you want.

2. Stretch fabric around the foam core.

3. Hot glue the fabric to the back of the foam core.

4. Wrap yarn tightly around the board, then tape to the back using a strong tape (like duct tape).

Pennant flags

1. Cut fabric into triangles using pinking shears.

2. Pin triangles to quilt binding tape.

3. Sew a straight line all the way down the tape. Remove pins as you go, taking care not to sew over them.

Q: My mom is letting me pick out some of my own clothes for the new school year. Help—I don't know where to start! I don't want to look like a dork.

A: Did you take the "What colors/season are you?" quiz on **page 54**? Try that, or just think about what colors you like. I'm a rainbow kind of guy, but a lot of people feel more comfortable dressing in monochromatic colors—a pale blue shirt with dark blue pants, or analogous colors—a yellow sweater with an orange skirt. Save your rainbow for a pop of color—a hair band, a necklace, or maybe bright, colorful shoelaces.

Q: I have to give a speech in school, and I'm really nervous. How can I feel more confident?

A: WEAR RED!
Red is a powerful color and will make you feel confident and in control. You will stand out and look energetic.

Make a COLOR CREATURE STUFFIE

YOU'LL NEED:

- Paper
- Pencil
- Ruler
- Fabric (felt or fabric of your choice)
- Thread or embroidery floss
- Sewing needle
- Pins
- Scissors
- Buttons or other embellishments
- Polyfill stuffing
- Sewing machine (optional)

Pick your colors and fabric. You can make your Color Creature stuffie out of felt or any fabric you like.

Here's another chance to use what you've learned about color. You can make these in any size. Use as a toy, pillow, or backpack decoration—or make one as a gift!

1. Pick a Color Creature stuffie from the patterns on page 61 (or design one of your own).

2. Decide what size you want to make it.

3. Use a grid to enlarge your design. Learn how on the next page.

This is a 1/2″ grid.

If you want your stuffie to be bright and have all the colors stand out, think about using <u>complementary colors</u>.

If you want it to be more subdued, think about using <u>analogous colors</u>.

If you want to use just one color along with tints, tones, and shades, think about using a <u>monochromatic color scheme</u>.

Use the color wheel to think about a color scheme.

Don't worry if your stuffie is not an exact copy of the original—just have fun drawing.

How to enlarge a pattern

You can enlarge the patterns on a copier, but we think it's more fun to enlarge a pattern using a grid.

1. Use a pencil and a ruler to draw grid lines 1/2″ apart on your stuffie pattern. Draw your lines going side to side as well as up and down, like in the picture. Number the rows, starting with 1. Letter the columns, starting with A.

2. Let's say you want to double your stuffie's size. Draw the same number of grid lines going up and down and side to side 1″ apart on a blank piece of paper to get squares. Number the rows and columns to match your original pattern.

3. Draw whatever you see in each square of your pattern on the bigger grid.

Purple Hare

Purple Hare

HiNT! ⟩ ⟩ ⟩

Put dots where the design crosses the grid lines.

FUNNY FaCes TO TRY:

heart nose	ninja	underbite	square nose
big cheeks	"x" marks the spot	mustache	three eyes
oval nose	pirate eye	monster mouth	no nose

Sewing your stuffie

1. Use the enlarged pattern to cut out all the pieces of your stuffie.

   Cut 2 pieces of each pattern:
   · 1 for the front side of the stuffie
   · 1 for the back side of the stuffie

2. Sew on all the pieces that will be on the front of the stuffie.

3. Sew together the two layers of arms, legs, and ears (if your stuffie has them). You will add them to your stuffie when you sew together the front and back sides.

4. Sew the front of the stuffie to the back with a straight stitch, but leave a 3″ hole open so you can stuff your stuffie. Add the arms, legs, and such as you get there.

5. Stuff your stuffie and then finish sewing him or her up.

> **IMPORTANT** You only need to cut 1 of each piece that is just decoration, like eyes, nose, and so on.

> You may need to use a few extra stitches to make sure the arms and legs stay attached.

HERE ARE A FEW STITCHES YOU CAN USE:

Straight stitch

(Great for sewing your stuffie pieces together)

Satin stitch
(Perfect for little noses)

French knot
(Maybe for eyes or belly buttons)

Cross stitch
(Cute decorative stitch)

Whip stitch
(Quick stitch to whip your stuffie together)

PATTERNS

Yellow Quack

Green Gurble

Purple Hare

Stormin' Blue

OK

Trace or copy this page
to use again and again.

61

Puzzle and quiz ANSWERS

Quick color quiz

(page 42)

Red and green are:
○ complementary colors

A color + white is:
○ a tint

Red, orange, and yellow are:
○ warm colors OR analogous colors

Yellow and violet are:
○ complementary colors

Dark green, green, and light green are:
○ monochromatic

A color + black is:
○ a shade

Green, yellow-green, and yellow are:
○ analogous colors

Red-violet and yellow-green are:
○ tertiary colors

Green, blue-green, and blue are:
○ cool colors OR analogous colors

A color + gray is:
○ a tone

Word find

(page 55)

D	A	D	A	K	S	F	K	S	R	P	P	P	A	T	W
F	B	D	D	X	D	S	D	W	T	H	R	S	A	E
H	L	C	K	O	E	D	A	H	S	J	I	R	H	R
U	U	J	G	M	F	O	R	A	U	S	M	D	Z	G
M	E	R	B	G	F	P	C	G	O	D	A	F	D	D
S	O	W	K	H	N	Y	D	H	I	W	R	I	F	G
G	V	A	S	E	C	O	N	D	A	R	Y	T	V	J
P	T	O	N	E	D	R	G	L	D	C	T	D	I	K
L	E	I	U	A	M	C	O	L	O	R	R	G	O	L
E	Q	A	N	U	D	X	H	O	R	S	G	T	L	G
Z	K	K	T	T	Z	A	J	O	R	A	N	G	E	B
Y	E	L	L	O	W	W	A	C	T	R	E	H	T	O
V	L	K	T	W	X	F	W	I	H	G	W	D	G	U
D	C	N	E	E	R	G	M	L	J	B	D	J	E	E
U	K	O	W	P	A	Y	C	F	M	X	C	W	U	R

How artists use color

(page 48)

1. Violet, red-violet, red, red-orange, and orange

2. Red and green, red-violet and yellow-green, violet and yellow

3. The complementary colors are:
red and green, yellow-orange and blue-violet, yellow and violet, and yellow-green and red-violet

The analogous colors are:
yellow-orange, yellow, yellow-green, green, blue-green, blue, blue-violet, violet, red-violet, and red

GLOSSARY >>>>>>

Acrylic paint A type of paint that washes off with soap and water when it's wet but is permanent when it dries. You can use it on paper or fabric. PAGE 14

Analogous colors A group of colors that are next to each other on the color wheel. Analogous colors always work well together. PAGE 32

Color plan Also known as a color scheme. A grouping of colors, such as monochromatic, analogous, or complementary groupings. PAGE 32

Color wheel A drawing with the primary, secondary, and sometimes tertiary colors placed in a circle or a ring. PAGE 10

Complementary colors Two colors that are opposite each other on the color wheel. Complementary color plans are lively and exciting. PAGE 32

Cool colors The colors of the water, sky, and ice: blues, greens, and violets. PAGE 36

Fabric paint A type of acrylic paint made especially to use on fabric. PAGE 44

Monochromatic A color plan that uses one color, including all that color's tints, tones, and shades. PAGE 32

Ombré [om-bray] Colors that blend from one to another. PAGE 26

Palette A surface used to hold and mix paint. It can be flat or have spaces called wells for the various colors. PAGE 14

Poster paint A type of paint that washes off with soap and water. It will run if it gets wet after it dries. Can be used on paper. PAGE 14

Primary colors Red, yellow, and blue. All other colors are made from these three colors. PAGE 12

Prism A transparent object that breaks light into the colors of the rainbow when white light shines through it. PAGE 8

Secondary colors Green, violet, and orange. They are created by mixing together two primary colors. PAGE 12

Shade A color + black. PAGE 22

Tertiary colors [ter-shee-err-ree] Red-violet, red-orange, blue-violet, blue-green, yellow-green, yellow-orange. Colors created by mixing a primary and a secondary color. PAGE 20

Tint A color + white. PAGE 22

Tone A color + gray. PAGE 22

Value The lightness or darkness of a color. PAGE 28

Warm colors The colors of the sun, fire, and heat: reds, oranges, and yellows. PAGE 36

Watercolors A type of paint that washes off with soap and water. They are not permanent, so you can't use them on fabric. PAGE 14

WORDS TO KNOW

About the AUTHORS

Lynn Mary Kerry

Lynn Koolish
Lynn lives a color-filled life in Berkeley, California, where she dyes fabric and makes quilts and other fiber art. She loves all the colors, so she can never decide what her favorite color is. As long as it's bright, she's happy. Sometimes she even dyes her hair purple. Lynn shares her love of color with others by teaching fabric-dyeing classes.

Mary Wruck
Mary loves art and everything creative! She has spent most of her career developing, marketing, and selling creative products. When she's not thinking up fun new things to help people express their creativity, you can find her hiking, camping, cooking, and playing with her daughter, husband, and dog. Mary lives in the San Francisco Bay Area of Northern California.

Kerry Graham
Kerry is a graphic designer and illustrator. During the day, as part of her job to develop new products, she gets to draw, sew, and surf the web for inspiration. When she's not in at work, she makes Girl Scout projects with her daughter, Alivia; dances hip-hop with her older son, Hudson; and cooks with her younger son, Trenton. Even though her life is busy, she is grateful every day for her family. She always makes the moments count. Kerry lives in the San Francisco Bay Area of Northern California.

EARNED A CERTIFICATE OF COLOR-OLGY

PLACE YOUR STICKER 1 THIS TRY

MEET ROY G. BV

Red Orange Yellow Green Blue Violet

ROY G. BV is a **mnemonic** (pronounced nih-mah-nik): an easy way to remember something.

In this case it's the order of the colors in the rainbow or on a color wheel.

OK

Trace or copy this page to use again and again.

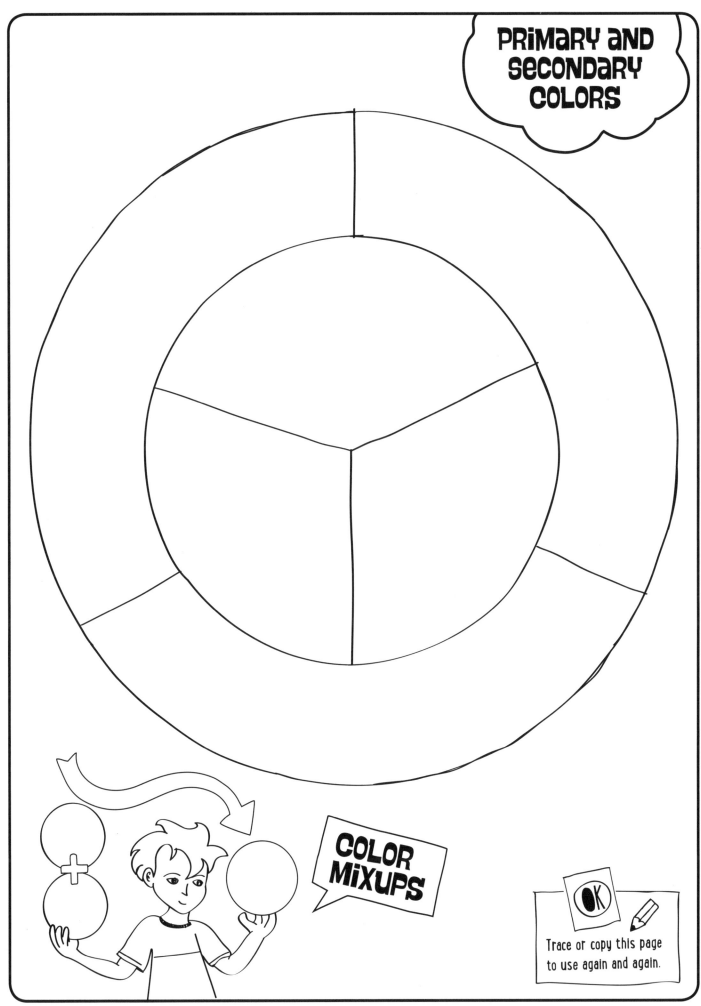

PRIMARY AND SECONDARY COLORS

COLOR MiXUPS

OK

Trace or copy this page to use again and again.

TiNTS, TONES, AND SHADES

WHITE + COLOR = TINT

COLOR + GRAY = TONE

COLOR + BLACK = SHADE

WHITE + COLOR = TINT

COLOR + GRAY = TONE

COLOR + BLACK = SHADE

Practice here.

OK

Trace or copy this page to use again and again.

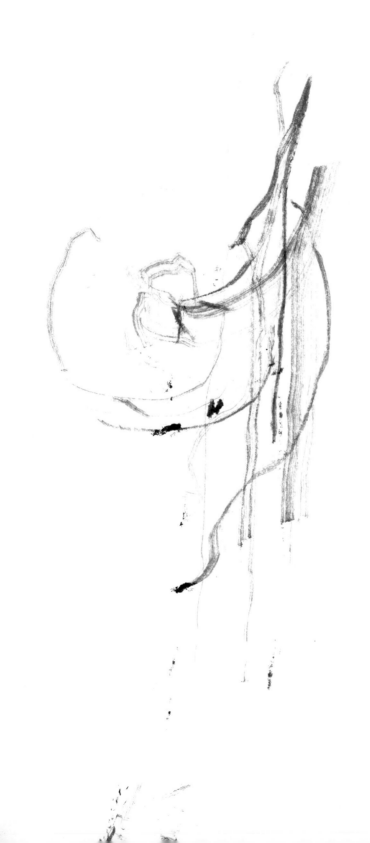

Value

Create an optical illusion.

OK
Trace or copy this page to use again and again.

Red + Green =

Violet + Yellow =

Blue + Orange =

COMPLEMENTARY
ANALOGOUS
MONOCHROMATIC

What happens when you mix complementary colors?

_____

Yellow-orange   Yellow   Yellow-green
Orange   Green
Red-orange   Blue-green
Red   Blue
Red-violet   Blue-violet
        Violet

Draw an arrow between a complementary color pair.

Color in the juggling balls with tints, tones, and shades of a monochromatic color scheme. Color in my jelly bean friends with analogous colors.

OK

Trace or copy this page to use again and again.

COOL

WARM

HOW COLORS AFFECT EACH OTHER

OK

Trace or copy this page to use again and again.

The PRIMARY COLORS are **red**, **yellow**, and **blue.**

Add two together and you get a SECONDARY COLOR.

Now mix a primary color with the secondary color that is next to it and you get a TERTIARY COLOR.

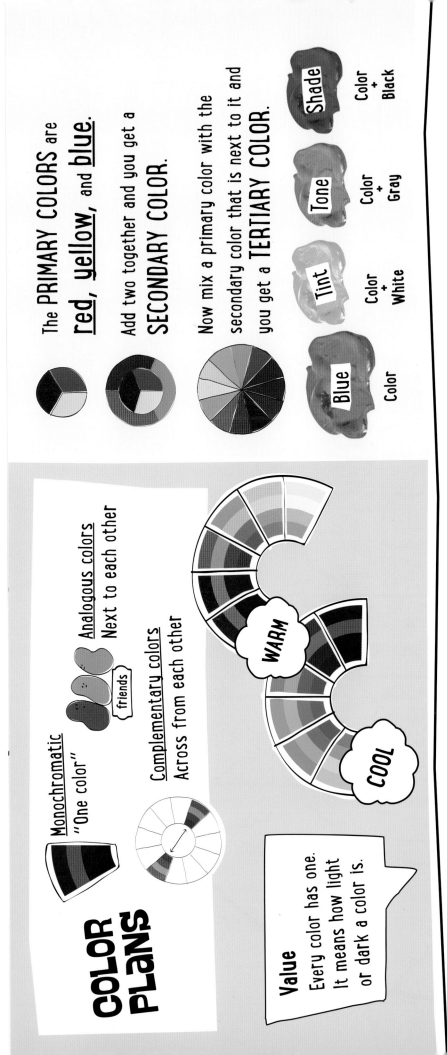

Blue
Color

Tint
Color + White

Tone
Color + Gray

Shade
Color + Black

COLOR PLANS

<u>Monochromatic</u>
"One color"

<u>Analogous colors</u>
Next to each other
{friends}

<u>Complementary colors</u>
Across from each other

WARM

COOL

Value
Every color has one. It means how light or dark a color is.

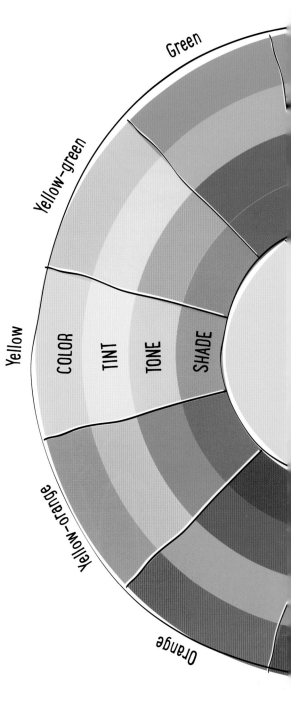

Green

Yellow-green

Yellow

Yellow-orange

Orange

COLOR

TINT

TONE

SHADE

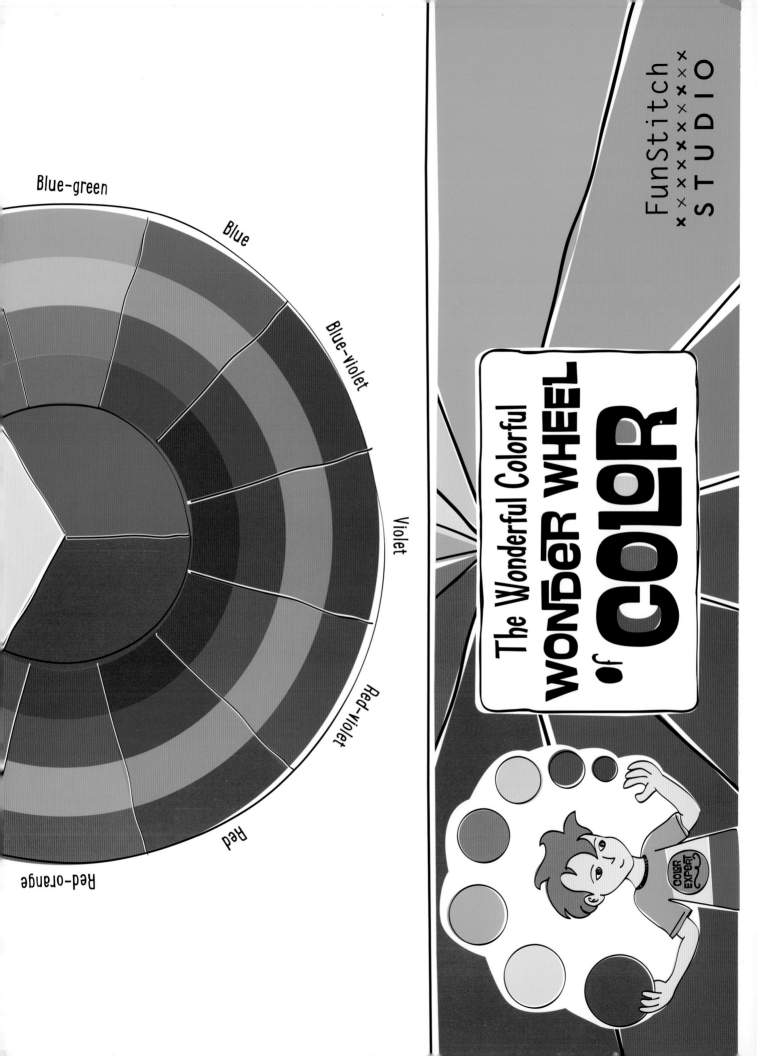